AT THE STARS

At the Stars

a play

MATTHEW MCCONKEY

Paperback ISBN: 9781965412381

Cover design by Jacob Arms

Produced in the United States
Published by Broken Tribe Review
Lawrence Landing Company
Raleigh, North Carolina 27609

Broken Tribe Press is a proud member of:
Independent Book Publishers Association
 and
Community of Literary Magazines and Presses

www.brokentribepress.com

BROKEN TRIBE PRESS DRAMA SERIES

For Heather

ACT I

Scene 1

Setting: Cemetery on a drizzling afternoon.

At Rise: Many people are standing at a graveside service, some with umbrellas. A man of faith can be heard lowly reciting Bible passages as words of comfort.

A man in a suit steps out from the crowd to address the audience. He is the man in the casket that the mourners came to see.

MATTHEW

My name is Matthew Morgan. I'm the man in the box these people have come to see. Did I expect to be here? No, not until I was at least in my seventies. I always thought death was for the old. But, even in life, we are in death, right? What got me? It was me slipping out of the shower.

You see, I'd taken a shower and when I stepped out, I slipped and fell, banging my head against the tub. I remember it hurt like hell. Normally, the rug would've been where I stepped out, but Carrie had taken all the rugs in the house to wash them. I don't blame her, though. I should've laid a towel down there in its place. Maybe it's not asking much just to have slipped and broke a leg or an arm. But to die from it? That's a little much, I think.

MATTHEW (Cont.)

All I remember after that is a headache and telling Carrie I had banged the hell out of my head. I laughed it off, but she was concerned about it. She even felt my head to see if there was a knot. There was. She told me I might want to have that looked at. I waved her off, telling her I had banged my head worse than that at work, which was true.

I brushed my teeth later that night, got into bed with my wife, and we lay there talking about what we were going to do on our week off from work. I was going to clean the gutters and cut the roses for the fall. Maybe watch a few college football games while she went to visit her sister in Collegedale for a few days. Nothing major. Just life as a middle-aged married couple whose kids are away at college.

I remember kissing my wife goodnight. I turned over to face the closet and closed my eyes. I never in a million years thought that would be our last kiss. Had I known, I would've never stopped kissing her. I would've held her in my arms all night long. But you never know when the last time is actually *the last time*. I sure am going to miss her. Will miss my sons. I'm going to miss all of this.

But it's cool to see those people behind me. I knew my wife, Carrie, and my two sons, Dylan and Raylan would be here. I even had some friends at work who showed up. My best friends, Danielle, Perry, Tommy, and Warren, are here as well. I knew that Danielle would be here, but Perry, Tommy, and Warren? I wasn't so sure. We haven't really spoken to each other for a long time. There wasn't any fight or anything like that. It was just old-fashioned life that got in the way. At any rate, still good to see them here.

End Scene 1

Act I

Scene 2

The man of faith concludes his reading at the graveside, and the crowd around the grave slowly disperses and walks away, mummering to themselves. Matthew Morgan stands still and allows the people to walk past him. He is an observer now.

(Off to the side, PERRY and WARREN walk slowly beside each other.)

PERRY

You good?

WARREN

I guess so. Just...just weird that one of us is gone now. You never know how you're going to feel when the first one dies, but I feel pretty weird right now.

PERRY

Yeah, me, too. I can't believe that Danielle showed; didn't expect that one.

WARREN

Me either. The last time I saw her was at my wedding twenty years ago.

PERRY

Same.

WARREN

She still looks good. Tommy has put on some weight, huh?

PERRY

We ain't exactly GQ models over here, my friend.

(The two men stop walking and look behind them as TOMMY and DANIELLE are trailing behind in what looks to be a conversation. The two of them walk over to PERRY and WARREN and stand for a conversation.)

TOMMY

Sucky day.

DANIELLE

Do we know what he died of? I didn't want to ask his wife. I bet it was a heart attack.

PERRY

Or a stroke. At our ages, it's one of the two in a situation like this. What do you think, Warren?

WARREN

(Shrugs) How the hell would I know?

PERRY

Well, you lived only six blocks from him and were his insurance agent...I just assumed that the two of you were still close.

WARREN

No. I guess we just never had the time. I don't know. We did have lunch together once.

TOMMY

Oh yeah? How long ago was that?

WARREN

Fifteen years ago, when I signed him to an insurance policy for his home and auto.

PERRY

It's a shame that we never got to know his wife and kids over there. Hell, for that matter, he never knew our families.

DANIELLE

What do we know about each other anymore? Probably not much of anything, I bet. All those years growing up around each other, and now we're nothing but strangers.

(The four of them stood and looked around, searching for the right words to add to what DANIELLE had just spoken. Nothing came for a few moments when PERRY asked a question.)

PERRY

Do you guys remember the time capsule? You guys remember us burying it, right?

(The four of them each stand silently for a few moments, reflecting on that day it was buried.)

TOMMY

Yeah, sure, man. We're supposed to dig it up after one of us dies.

(Again, more silence from the group for a few moments.)

PERRY

We'll take it to the lake house and see what's in there once
we get it. I don't remember anything we put in there that
day.

DANIELLE

Didn't we bury it in your backyard back in the summer of
1992? *(Looks at WARREN)*

WARREN

No, it was July of 1991, and it was in Tommy's backyard.

TOMMY

I remember when Matthew came up with that idea. He
made us take our most prized possessions and put them in
this metal box, a time capsule, he called it.

DANIELLE

You think it's still there?

TOMMY

Should be. But my mom doesn't live there anymore. She
hasn't since twenty years ago, I reckon.

PERRY

So, it's been in the ground, what, thirty-five plus years?
You guys think it's intact?

WARREN

I would imagine it's still intact as the day we put it in the
ground.

DANIELLE

I don't remember what I put in there.

PERRY

Me either.

TOMMY

No clue. Hell, I can barely remember yesterday.

> *(After a few moments of silence between the group, PERRY speaks.)*

PERRY

Okay then. So, we dig up the box, bring it to the lake house, and open it.

WARREN

Yeah, I've got a few hours to spend. Why not.

PERRY

Tommy?

TOMMY

Yeah, man. I'll go over to my old house and talk to the new owners, tell them what's going on. Maybe they'll let me dig in the yard. Warren, you coming with me? (Warren nods)

PERRY

Danielle? You in on a trip down memory lane?

DANIELLE

(Stands there and considers for a few moments while her friends watch her silently.)

I've really got to get back home. It's a five-hour drive ahead of me, and I've got to work tomorrow.

(She breaks away from the group. Wiping her eyes, she turns to the group.)

It was great seeing all of you; really, it was. And good luck with that time capsule. Message me on Facebook, and let me know what I have in there. I don't even remember what I put in there.

(DANIELLE exits the stage out of sight.)

(The three men stand there looking at each other and then watch DANIELLE walk away across the cemetery.)

PERRY

Well, that's the last we'll see of her. Her and Matthew were super close and crazy about each other back then. If she won't do this with us, she ain't coming back when one of us dies.

TOMMY

You don't know that.

PERRY

Yeah, I do. We're not the same group we were thirty-something years ago, man.

WARREN

Listen, before we get into this existential crisis, Perry, you go to the lake house, and me and Tommy will go get the box. We'll call if there's a problem.

(The three men exit the stage.)

End Scene 2

Act I

Scene 3

Inside Warren's car with Tommy. Warren is driving, while Tommy looks down at his phone in the passenger seat. The two have been silent since the cemetery. Warren breaks the silence with a question as he clears his throat.

WARREN

I can't believe that he's gone.

TOMMY

(Looking down at his phone, he answers)

 Yeah...I was pretty shocked to hear about it myself. Forty-eight is too young to turn off the lights. Remember David McGee? He was what? Thirty-four when he died.

WARREN

 Yeah, I remember David. He was a hell of a softball player, wasn't he?

TOMMY

(Still with his head lowered, scrolling on his phone in the passenger seat)

Yup. Could hit a ball a country mile, that's for sure. And man, could he play the hot corner.

WARREN

How many kids did he leave behind? Two?

TOMMY

Ummmmm...I think he had three: two girls and a boy.

WARREN

Matthew's family seemed to be taking it rough.

TOMMY
(Still scrolling on his phone)
Yeah, they've got a long road ahead of them. Death ain't easy on any level. I remember when Dad died. That stunned us all.

WARREN

Your dad died? When? *(A voice of surprise)*

TOMMY
(Still scrolling with his head down)
Oh...about eight years back.

WARREN

Why didn't I know about it? Should've called me.

TOMMY

Warren, I don't want to break the news to you...
(Raises his head and looks at Warren)

But our group of friends ain't the best in the world at keeping up with each other. What about your parents? How are they?

WARREN

Dad has Alzheimer's, and Mom is taking care of him. But she can barely take care of herself. My sister helps some, and so do I. But Dad is getting to the point where he's going to have to be put into assisted living.

TOMMY

Sorry to hear that, man. Your dad was really cool back in the day. I remember we'd be at your house shooting basketball and he'd come out and school us in Horse.

WARREN
(Laughs)
Yeah, Dad was a great shot. He'd always tell me stories about how good he was in school.
(Warren continues to drive as a few moments of silence slip between the two friends before he speaks)

I feel like trash coming to see him dead. I mean, I could make time for that, but I couldn't make the time while he was alive.

TOMMY
(Looking out the passenger side window and then through the windshield)

Don't beat yourself up too badly. You weren't the only one. I never checked in with him either. The last time I saw him was six years ago at Food City. Me and Abby were in there buying some charcoal and paper plates for a cookout, and we ran into him and his wife. Lord, we must've stayed in that aisle and talked a good forty minutes catching up. We added each other on Facebook after that. But other than liking posts, that was about the extent of our relationship. It's kind of sad when you think about it, especially considering how close we all were growing up.

WARREN
You never have friends like the ones you had when you were growing up, do you?

TOMMY

No, you certainly do not. So, what about you?

WARREN

What about me?

TOMMY

I saw on Facebook that your son graduated from college during the summer. You just have the one kid, right?

WARREN

Yeah, just Jake. Me and Amy didn't want any more after him, mainly because of how hard her pregnancy was. She liked to have died. So, we didn't want to chance it. Jake came out healthy, and we thought, ' Why risk it? '

But yeah, he graduated from college and is working at Lowe's home office in HR. Seems to like it pretty good, I guess. What about you? Three kids I've seen on Facebook?

TOMMY

April, June, and August. All girls, all named after the months they were born in.

WARREN

I bet raising girls is a trip.

TOMMY

You got that right. Not for the faint of heart, that's for sure. Raising daughters takes a certain kind of patience and gentleness. But each of my girls is different. I couldn't talk to April the same way I did June, and I couldn't talk to August the way I did April. They were all different and required a different type of parenting.

WARREN

I think Amy, deep down, wanted to try one more time and maybe have a daughter. But the risks were just too big. Makes you wonder how much our lives would've changed with two kids, a boy and a girl.

TOMMY

Who knows? One little thing can change your entire trajectory. How's the insurance biz?

WARREN

Good. Good. Kind of boring, if I'm being honest. Not what I wanted to do when I grew up.

TOMMY

Tell me about it. Being a machinist at BribCo wasn't on my list either.

WARREN

How long have you been there?

TOMMY

Fifteen long years. I make good money, but working on machines on assembly lines is not what I wanted to do with my life.

WARREN

Very few people are doing what they want with their lives. I wonder if Matthew was doing what he wanted with his?

TOMMY
(Considers for a few moments)
I don't know. He told me he was a Pepsi vendor for all the stores around the area. Made pretty good from what I understand. But was he happy with what he was doing for a living? Hell, are any of us?

WARREN

I think we find something that we can tolerate. Maybe that's what life really is...just tolerating stuff until you die. How long have you been married?

TOMMY

Twenty-five years. You?

WARREN

Twenty-two. We've had our ups and downs, but we've managed not to kill each other.

TOMMY

Same. I remember Heather Gray in high school. Man, everyone thought you two would end up married someday.

WARREN (Laughs)

Yeah, man, she was something else. The love of my young life. Lost my virginity to her. During high school, she was everything to me.

TOMMY

What happened to ya'll?

WARREN

After we graduated, she went to college and met some guy. She broke up with me in summer of '98. Damn near killed me. But six months later, I met Amy, and the rest is history.

TOMMY

First loves. God, I remember mine. Connie Brackett.

WARREN

I remember her. Wasn't she a grade ahead of us?

TOMMY

Yeah, she was a sophomore when we were freshmen. I met her in Physical Science class. God, she was awesome.

WARREN

I remember you two were an item back then. What happened?

TOMMY

We were. But then she graduated and started hanging out with these older guys from Tape City, where she worked. I told her that I didn't like it, but she said that it was my problem. We basically stopped talking, and then she got pregnant by some dude there, and that was that.

WARREN

You know, I always thought Matthew and Danielle would end up together.

TOMMY

I did too. I wonder why they didn't.

WARREN

How do we know they didn't? They could've done it in secret, and we'd never known.

TOMMY
(Laughs)
Matthew would've told us. That kid never could keep a secret.

WARREN

True, but what if? I remember once me and Danielle were out in town shooting basketball behind the bank in the lot. I just came out and asked her if she would date Matthew.

TOMMY

What did she say?

WARREN

She said she thought he was awesome, but she didn't want to ruin their friendship.

TOMMY

I do remember that time in our junior year when she was dating Jeremy Boxer, the guy on the football team.

WARREN

Yup, and Matthew was crushed. How long did they date? Six months?

TOMMY

I don't know. Sounds about right. All I knew was that Matthew moped around the whole time. Danielle wasn't around us much during that time either. But then again, none of us were around each other much. We were all too busy working jobs.

WARREN

God, ain't that right. I hated working at Taco Bell. Worst job I ever had. Zero stars.

TOMMY

Ace Hardware was no better. Especially in the spring, when people would come in wanting paint mixed. They would talk to me like I was stupid and didn't know how. I literally used a formula that the machine told me to use and mixed it. I think that job was where my hatred for people first started. (*Both laugh*)

Hey, you found my old house (*surprised*)

WARREN

Hey, you never forget where your best friends lived or their phone numbers.

TOMMY

Okay, hot shot, what was my home ph...

WARREN

471-3291...Now let's go up and knock on the front door, and look like complete idiots.

End Scene 3

Act I

Scene 4

Inside Danielle's SUV. She sits behind the steering wheel, crying. Matthew is sitting in the passenger seat, staring through the windshield at the audience.

MATTHEW
You seriously not going to the lake house to see what is in that time capsule?

DANIELLE
(*Wipes her eyes and looks over at the ghost and then sniffles, looking out the windshield at the audience*)
No, I don't want to.

MATTHEW
Well, that's just stupid.

DANIELLE
No, you know what stupid is? You being dead.
> (*Says this with emotion as her voice cracks at the word DEAD*)
> (*Silence between the two for a few moments*)

MATTHEW
It's not like I planned to die, you know?

(More silence as DANIELLE sniffles, sobbing here and there)

DANIELLE

We just didn't have enough time.

MATTHEW

Danielle, honey, there was *never* going to be enough time, not for us. You remember when we first met? Huh?

DANIELLE
(Wipes her eyes and stares out the windshield that looks across the audience)

Yeah. It was sixth grade. We had just moved into town from Louisiana. I was sitting alone in the lunchroom, and you and the boys came over and asked if it was okay to sit and have lunch there.

MATTHEW
(Smiles and nods)

Yup. I remember seeing you by yourself for that whole week at recess and during lunch, and I told the boys that if you hadn't made any friends by Friday, we were going to come over and sit with you.

DANIELLE

And you guys were the best friends I ever had growing up.

MATTHEW

I wouldn't have changed a thing—none of it. You were my best friend. Always. And I'm sorry that I died. I am. I know that things have changed now—all the plans...gone.

DANIELLE

This whole situation is not fair.

MATTHEW

Life ain't fair. Look at me...cut down in my forties. This is not how I thought my life would end. Never once. I honestly thought I'd die as an old man in my nineties. It's what my dad told me once. Guess he was wrong.

DANIELLE
(*Sniffles more, wipes her eyes once again, and lays her head on the steering wheel*)

Now, I've got to live the rest of my life without...
(*She starts to cry as MATTHEW sits there and watches*)

MATTHEW

Listen, I know you're hurt, and I hate seeing you in pain. Remember that time out on the basketball court during the summer of '93, right before we went to high school? You got hit in the face by that pass from Jessie? Bloodied your nose pretty good. We thought you broke it. Remember?

DANIELLE
(*Crying, nods*)

Yeah, I remember.

MATTHEW

I remember taking my Michael Jordan jersey off and holding it to your nose to stop the bleeding. And what did I tell you once I got you calmed down?

DANIELLE
(*Raises her head from the steering wheel and wipes her eyes again*)

That it would be okay.

MATTHEW

Right. And this...this is going to be okay, too. Eventually. Listen, I know you want to leave. I know that you want to go home and just sink. But I think those guys need you at that lake house today. I also think you need to see what's inside that box. You might be glad you stayed.

DANIELLE

I don't know if I can, Matthew. I really don't. I mean... everything that has happened before your...and now you're...you're gone. Like, gone.
> (*Lowers head on her steering wheel and starts to cry again*)

MATTHEW

I know. And I wish there were some way I could fix all of this and ease your pain. But I can't. I think it would be therapeutic for you to go to Perry's lake house and see the guys, reconnect just for a bit, and open that box.

DANIELLE
> (*Long pause, DANIELLE crying, mumbling incoherently. MATTHEW stares at her. Eventually, DANIELLE wipes her eyes and stares out the windshield*)

I can't go back. There's a memory there of us I don't want to feel again. Not after today.
> (*DANIELLE pauses*)
I think what's best for me is to head back home and put some miles between everything. Maybe get my head right. I'm sorry...I just can't go back.

Blackout, end ACT I

Act II

Scene 1

1991. Inside Wilson's Drugstore: Thirteen-year-olds Perry, Matthew, Danielle, Warren, and Tommy are crammed into a booth. On one side of the booth seat sits Danielle, who is sitting against the full-view glass window that looks out onto the town's street. Matthew is sitting close to her, and Tommy is on the other end.

Perry and Warren sit across the table from them on the other side of the booth.

Perry and Warren are flipping through the comic books they had just bought. Matthew and Danielle are sitting close together, sharing a Pepsi while Tommy is cleaning his fingernails with a pocketknife.

No talking was going on amongst the group until Matthew cleared his throat and spoke.

MATTHEW
You know what would be cool?

PERRY
Having sex with your mom?

MATTHEW

No, as much as it would be with yours...but I'm serious.

PERRY

So was I.
>(*He laughs and elbows WARREN, who looks up from his comic book, bothered*)

MATTHEW

I was watching this news thing the other night, and it was about these people who buried a time capsule.

PERRY

Like the type where they put stuff in it from current times and then open it like thirty years later or something?

TOMMY

Or is it like the type where they put stuff in it from current times and then open it like thirty years later or something?
(*Everyone laughs*)

PERRY

I hate you!

MATTHEW

But Tommy's right.

PERRY

Hey, I said it first. He just said what I said.

TOMMY

Shut up, Matthew's trying to tell us something. (*TOMMY laughs*)

MATTHEW

What I'm saying is that I think it would be neat if we did something like that. You know, something we could come back and dig up later.

WARREN

If I'm still around here in this town for thirty years, please kill me.

DANIELLE

I think that's a way cool idea. We could each put something valuable to us in it.

TOMMY

Warren, how are we going to fit your virginity in a box? (*Everyone laughs*)

MATTHEW

I think Danielle is right. We each think about what we're going to put in that box. Make sure it's something valuable, though, something that will make us smile when we see it again.

PERRY

When would you like to open this time capsule? Twenty-five years? Thirty?

MATTHEW
(*Ponders the question*)

When the first person in our group right here dies.
(*Everyone looks at each other. Even WARREN takes his eyes from his comic book and looks around the booth*)

WARREN

Are you serious? When one of us dies?

MATTHEW

Why not? I think it'll mean more to us that way.

TOMMY

What happens if one of us dies in a few years? What then?

MATTHEW

We open it. But I don't think any of us are going to die anytime soon. (Group sits and ponders)

DANIELLE

I'm in.

TOMMY

Why not.

PERRY

Yup, let's do it.

WARREN

I think it'll be cool. I'm in.

TOMMY

We could bury it in my backyard if you guys want to.

MATTHEW
(*Nods*)
Works for me. What would you guys put in it?

(*Everyone sits quietly and thinks it over*)

PERRY

A box of condoms.

TOMMY

Yeah, because you ain't ever going to need them.

PERRY
No, because your mom is allergic to latex. (*Everyone laughs*)

MATTHEW
Seriously, though, let's all think about it.

WARREN
When do we want to do this?

DANIELLE
Saturday afternoon? (*Everyone nods in agreement*)

MATTHEW
Okay, cool. I'll take care of the box. Dad has a pretty good-sized metal box with these latches in his shed that would work out good for us, I think. I'll work out all the other stuff we'll need. Just think about what you're putting in it.

(*Everyone nods*)

End Scene 1

Act II

Scene 2

Saturday afternoon. Matthew, age 13, is in his dad's work shed while his dad is listening to the Atlanta Braves game on the radio. His dad is sitting on a stool over his workbench, reading the newspaper as Matthew comes in.

Matthew is prowling around the shed while his dad keeps his eyes on the paper and his ears on the game. Matthew keeps prowling in all corners of the tool shed when his dad turns the page and watches his son for a few moments.

MATTHEW'S DAD
Son, what is it that you're looking for?

MATTHEW
UMM...I'm looking for that medium-sized metal box you had. *(Mimics the size with his hands)*

MATTHEW'S DAD
I don't have a metal box like that.

MATTHEW
Yeah, you do. It's got two silver latches on it and it's this big. I saw it here a few months ago. Still got to be in here...somewhere.

MATTHEW'S DAD
I don't know what you're talking about. And what do you
want with it anyway?

MATTHEW
(Still searching, frustrated)
I just need it. Me and my friends are needing it for
something.

MATTHEW'S DAD
*(He folds his newspaper and lays it
down on the table, and looks under his
stool where the kneehole is under the
table. He uses his feet and slides a metal
box over to him. He gets off the stool and
bends down to pick it up. It's the
medium-sized metal box.)*
Is this it?

MATTHEW
*(From the far end of the tool shed,
MATTHEW sees it and smiles, walking
over to his dad)*

Yeah, this is it...told you it was in here. Care if I have it?

*(Takes it from his dad and puts it on the
worktable, and flips open the latches to
inspect inside it.)*

MATTHEW'S DAD
Yeah, I reckon you can. I didn't even know I had it. Come
to think of it, I don't even know where it came from. Nice
looking box though, ain't it?

MATTHEW

Yup. Exactly what I need too.

MATTHEW'S DAD

So, what are you up to?

MATTHEW

Well, me and my friends are doing a time capsule. We're going to put stuff that we love in here and bury it.

MATTHEW'S DAD

So, you and your friends will dig it back up in, say, twenty or thirty years? Something like that?

MATTHEW

Sort of. But not exactly. We're going to open it up when the first one of the group dies. *(Silence)*
I know that it sounds kinda morbid, but it makes sense, I guess, to me.

MATTHEW'S DAD
                    *(Sits back down on the stool,
                    arms folded across his chest)*

Well, yeah, it does. But I can see why. When that day happens and all of ya'll come back to dig it up, it's going to evoke all kinds of memories of the times you're having right now. But, of course, when that time does come, and I hope it's very, very far away, you're going to remember these days right here with vivid flashes of times forgotten.

MATTHEW

Wow, is this how you talk to your college
students? *(Both laugh)*

MATTHEW'S DAD

Sometimes. So, what brought this on? This time capsule?

MATTHEW

I don't really know. I saw a news thing the other night where these people did it, and I thought it would be cool. But I didn't want there to be a set date when we went back to dig it up. I wanted there to be a reason to dig it up.

MATTHEW'S DAD

And what better way to mark something like a death.

MATTHEW
(Nods)

Right. I know it sounds Edgar Allan Poe-ish, but I think we'll be glad we did it this way when that day comes. Well, one of us won't know at all. You ever think about dying?

MATTHEW'S DAD
(Sits there on his stool for a few moments, head down in thought, arms still folded around his chest in a relaxed state)

I used to, son. I did. Back when I was in the war, fighting in the jungles of Vietnam against an unseen enemy, I wondered if I would live to see the next hour. Sometimes you just never knew. I was 18, not much older than you are right now, fighting in a war that I was forced to go into and fighting for something that I had no idea what it was over.

I thought about death so much back then. For eighteen months, the thought dominated my life, hour by hour, day by day. But I swore to myself that if I survived my deployment, I would come home and never think about death again. And I haven't. Over there, I was around death so much that I couldn't help but keep it at the forefront of my thoughts. I think it's what kept me on my toes, kept me vigilant. I don't know.

Have you been thinking about death?

MATTHEW

Not much, but it has crossed my mind some.

MATTHEW'S DAD

Well, son, I'm going to tell you something. We never know when the hour of our death is at hand. But I want you to listen to me. You've got a long, long time to live.

MATTHEW

You think so?

MATTHEW'S DAD
(Smiles, and playfully smacks the bill of his son's Braves hat on his head)

Yes, at least until you are in your 90s. But never rule out a random accident like slipping, getting out of the shower, or breaking your neck on a bicycle. Sometimes you just never know. But I honestly think you're going to be a very old man when that day comes.

MATTHEW

I hope so, Dad.

MATTHEW'S DAD

Enough with the talk of death. What are you going to put into this box?

MATTHEW

I don't know exactly. I've got a few things picked out. But I haven't decided just yet. What would you have put in a time capsule back when you were a kid?

MATTHEW'S DAD
(Sits there on his stool and considers his son's question)

There was a picture of me and my dad back in 1965. I was 13, just like you. I was in my baseball uniform, and my dad was in his shirt and tie. Our arms were around each other, and we were smiling. I don't know where that picture ever got off to, and man, oh, man, I wish I had it now. I'd like to see the old man and me again.

It was the only picture of him and me that was ever made. We weren't a photographic family by any means. But if I had something to put in a time capsule, it would be that picture so I could see it once again and remember that day, what he looked like, instead of seeing him in my mind.

MATTHEW
I want to put something in there that means something. Like, if I were the first to go, I want my friends to see it and say, 'This must've meant the world to him.'

MATTHEW'S DAD
(Smiles and leans forward on his stool and hugs his son)

You're one in a billion, Kiddo—one in a billion.

End Scene 2

Act II

Scene 3

1991. Outside in Tommy's backyard. The five friends are looking around, trying to decide where to bury the metal box. DANIELLE is propped up on a shovel, MATTHEW is holding the metal box, WARREN is holding a thick sheet of plastic, and PERRY is talking out loud about where the best place would be to bury the box.

PERRY

It needs to be someplace where we don't forget where it's at.

TOMMY

I don't think we'll forget where we put it.

PERRY

We might. Who knows how long it will be until we all come back. It might be 50 years. Your folks may not even live here by that time.

MATTHEW

What about over there? *(Points in a direction)*

PERRY

Nah, I don't think that looks like a great place.

WARREN

What about over here?

PERRY

Nah, too many bushes.

DANIELLE

Here's an idea. It's Tommy's backyard, let him decide.
Tommy? What do you think?
> *(TOMMY looked around his
> backyard and considered for a
> few moments)*

TOMMY

Over there by the willow tree. That will be perfect, I think.

MATTHEW
> *(Everyone stood there and
> thought it over and nodded)*

Yeah, that'll be perfect—a good marker for when we come
back.

PERRY

What happens if the willow gets cut down or a storm
takes it or...

MATTHEW, DANIELLE, TOMMY, WARREN

Shut up, Perry!
> *(MATTHEW walks across the
> yard toward the willow tree with
> the metal box in tow. He goes
> over to the trunk, turns around,
> and paces twenty-five steps
> toward TOMMY's house)*

MATTHEW

Right here is where we'll bury it—twenty-five steps from
the trunk of the willow tree towards Tommy's
house. *(Everyone nodded)*

Danielle, bring the shovel, and we'll start to dig.

PERRY

Why so far away from the tree?

MATTHEW

Roots. Don't want to dig into those. I think this far out
here will be safe from all that.

*(The four kids walk across to stand where MATTHEW is
holding the box)*

End Scene 3

Act II

Scene 4

Adult TOMMY and WARREN are standing on Tommy's old front porch. TOMMY knocks on the front door of his old house. A few moments later, an older woman opens the front door cautiously.

                    OLDER WOMAN
                    (Apprehensive)
Can I help you, gentlemen?

                    TOMMY
Hi there, my name is Tommy Baker. I grew up in this house years ago. And I have an odd question for you.

                    OLDER WOMAN
  Okay?

                    TOMMY
You see, back in 1991, me and my friends buried a time capsule in my backyard—well, your backyard now. Now, one of our friends died, and we're supposed to dig it up. Is there any way we can do that?

OLDER WOMAN
Wow.. Okay, sure, go ahead. Whereabouts is it at?

TOMMY
Close to the willow tree.

OLDER WOMAN
We had that cut down about 15 years ago after the big storm.

TOMMY
(TOMMY and WARREN look at each other)

Well, I remember where it was. So, it shouldn't be a problem. So...

OLDER WOMAN
Oh, sure, sure. Just do what you men need to do. All I ask is that you fill in any holes you make. I've got grandkids that play back there, and I don't need them to break a leg or ankle.

TOMMY
Yeah, no problem. Thanks so much for your help.

> *(TOMMY and WARREN walk off the front porch, the woman closes the door, and over to the side of the house, the two men look out into the backyard)*

I think it's over there if I remember right. God, it's been so long since I was here, it doesn't even look the same.

WARREN
Looks smaller. Why does everything look smaller when you come back?

TOMMY

I don't know, but that's true, though. Back then, the world seemed bigger. Now, it's smaller. *(Exhales)*

We'd better get to digging and get this over with.

WARREN
(TOMMY starts walking where the willow tree used to be when WARREN calls to him)

Hey, wait. We don't have shovels. And we'll need to buy a bag or two of topsoil to fill in the holes.
(TOMMY turns around and puts his arms in the air in a 'are you kidding me gesture')

I can't believe we didn't think about that. I guess we're going to the hardware store then. I'll tell the lady we'll be back.

End Scene 4

Act II

Scene 5

1991. Tommy's backyard. TOMMY, WARREN, and PERRY are digging the hole while MATTHEW and DANIELLE are shooting basketball across the yard.

PERRY and TOMMY watch as WARREN is digging the hole, and TOMMY looks over at MATTHEW and DANIELLE.

TOMMY
You think they'll ever get together?

PERRY
Who knows with those two? But you can tell they like each other.

TOMMY
I asked Matthew a few weeks ago about it, and he said they were just friends. But I don't believe that.

PERRY
Yeah, I've asked him about it, too. I asked Danielle last week when we were out riding bikes. She said the same thing. But I don't know about it. I think there's a spark there.

TOMMY

I think so, too. You think they've done it?

WARREN

Hell no!

> (Over at the basketball goal, DANIELLE
> and MATTHEW are talking and
> shooting basketball)

MATTHEW

Just a couple more months and we're off to high school.
(Shoots the ball)

DANIELLE

> (Grabs the ball and bounces it a few
> times before she shoots)

Yeah, not looking forward to it.

MATTHEW

> (Gets the ball and dribbles it
> around and then shoots)

Me either. The next four years are going to be crazy. Can
you believe we're going to be in high school, though?
Seems like life is going by fast.

DANIELLE

> (Takes the ball and walks it back as she
> dribbles)

I used to hear that when I was younger. Maybe it's true.
(Shoots)

MATTHEW

> (Gets the rebound and walks it around
> dribbling)

I think it is. So, um, Dale Dexter told me he liked you the
other day.

DANIELLE

He didn't?! *(Laughs)* Oh my God. No way! That guy is a total creep.

MATTHEW
(Shoots the ball and misses. DANIELLE runs over and gets the ball and dribbles around)

Yeah, he sure did. Told me in history class.

DANIELLE

What did you tell him?

MATTHEW

I told him that you were madly in love with him.

(Laughs as DANIELLE throws the basketball at him as she laughs, chasing him)

DANIELLE

You better not have!

(Over from where the boys are digging, PERRY calls for MATTHEW and DANIELLE to come over. They trot over and all five of them stand before the hole in the ground)

PERRY

Okay, hole is dug, no thanks to you two. *(Looks at MATTHEW and DANIELLE)*

DANIELLE

How deep is it?

TOMMY

I'd say about two feet.

MATTHEW

Okay. Well, if everyone is good with what they've put into this box, then it's ready to be wrapped and buried.

> *(WARREN takes the thick plastic sheeting and wraps the metal box up several times, making it water secure)*

Tommy, since it's your yard, you care to do the honors and put it into the ground?

> *(TOMMY takes the box wrapped in plastic and gets down on his knees, putting it securely into the hole.) He rises back up on his feet as they all look down at it)*

Now, when the first one of us dies, this box comes back out and the survivors open it.

TOMMY

You and Danielle can cover it up, me and the boys are going to get something to drink and shoot some ball.

> *(The boys walk away, leaving MATTHEW and DANIELLE standing at the hole)*

MATTHEW

You think this is morbid?

DANIELLE

Yeah. But that's what makes this so cool. I mean, I don't want any of us to die, but when that day comes, it'll be neat to open it up and see what we buried when we were kids. It'll be like touching the past.

MATTHEW
(Takes the shovel and starts covering up the hole with the mound of dirt that was made)

Yeah, I think so too. 'Touching the past', I like that.

DANIELLE
I just made that line up in my head. *(Laughs)*

MATTHEW
(Still shoveling)
Great line. Needs to be in a book one day. So, that was a no on Dale? We never finished that conversation.

DANIELLE
God no! *(Laughs)* I can't believe that you put your Braves hat in that box.

MATTHEW
Well, it had to be our most prized possession, right? And that hat is mine. I got it at a baseball game when I was in fourth grade. It's been my trademark ever since. Besides, I've got another one at home, but that one in there...that one is my most cherished item. Maybe I'll be able to get it back one day.

DANIELLE
So, I heard from Stacy Kinderbox that you and Marcy Pendergrass have been passing notes around to each other.

MATTHEW
(Still shoveling)
Yeah, but nothing major. She's too upper-class for me. Not my style. Besides, I like someone else.

DANIELLE

Oh really? She must be a great girl to get your attention.

MATTHEW

(Continues shoveling)

Oh, she is. A complete knockout. Perfect for me in every way. She makes me laugh, we have the same tastes in movies and music. She's the Morticia to my Gomez.

DANIELLE

That's so weird because I've been having this crush on a guy for a bit now, but don't know if I should say anything or not.

MATTHEW

(Continues to shovel)

Oh yeah? What's he like?

DANIELLE

Super cute. Can't shoot a basketball for nothing, but I don't hold that against him, you know. I do play for the school and have a distinct advantage over him in skill. But he likes all the movies and music I like, and he's deep and funny. He has this cute thing he does when he's thinking. He'll bite his lower lip when he's in thought. He's the Gomez to my Morticia.

MATTHEW

(Finishes shoveling and pats the dirt with the back side of the shovel)

Well, he sounds pretty amazing. What are the chances of you two getting together, you think?

DANIELLE

I don't know. Good, I hope. What about your chances with yours?

MATTHEW

Like yours, good. Actually, I think better than good. I just got to stop being scared and ask her.

DANIELLE

Why are you scared of her?

MATTHEW

I don't want to ruin a friendship if things go bad.

DANIELLE

I get that. You think things would go bad—I mean, with you and this girl?

MATTHEW

I don't think so. But what if we do this and it ends badly? Not only do we lose a relationship, but we also lose a friendship. That's two hits at once.

DANIELLE

How about we don't have any crazy expectations and just let it do what it's going to do? Like, have fun with it.

MATTHEW
(Stands there propped up on the shovel thinking, looking at DANIELLE)
Do we keep it from the guys?

DANIELLE

I think so. At least for the time being. No sense in dragging them in on it. Maybe later on, if things progress.

MATTHEW

Square deal.
(The guys come walking over to where DANIELLE and MATTHEW are at the covered hole)

MATTHEW (Cont.)
Hey, later tonight, I thought you and me could go down to
the park to look at the stars. I mean, if you want to, that is.

DANIELLE
(Giggles)
Why, Matthew Morgan, are you asking me on a date?

MATTHEW
(Stands there with his shovel looking at
her and then grins)
Yeah, I guess I am.

DANIELLE
(Smiles and nods)
That'll be fun.

PERRY
Everything good?

MATTHEW
Yup, it's covered up until one of us dies.

PERRY
Let's go to Pappa Enzo's and get some pizza and play some
pinball. Warren's buying.

WARREN
I ain't got that much money to cover everyone.

PERRY
Just get it from your mom. I gave her twenty last night.

WARREN
Not funny!...wait, that kinda was.

End Scene 5

Act II

Scene 6

Lakehouse. Daytime. Current time. PERRY walks to the dock behind the house and sees a woman sitting at the edge, looking off into the distance of the lake.

DANIELLE sits at the edge of the dock facing the audience.

He walks down the dock and sits down beside her.

DANIELLE jumps, scared, and lets out a shriek. She takes her earbuds out as PERRY sits down beside her.

PERRY
Sorry, I thought you heard me coming. You okay?

DANIELLE
Yeah, yeah, I'm good. You scared me, is all. I guess I was in my own little world listening to "Plainsong."

PERRY
If memory serves, that was the song you and Matthew slow-danced to here that night we graduated, right?

DANIELLE

That would be the one. God, this place looks the same. It even smells the same out here.

PERRY

Yeah, it does. There have been a few minor changes inside the lake house since all of us were here on graduation night, but mostly it's the same. So, elephant in the room. I didn't think you were coming back. I thought we'd seen the last of you at the cemetery.

DANIELLE
(Silence)

I felt that I owed it to him to be here. I didn't want to break a promise we all made back when we were kids.

PERRY
(Nods)

Yeah, me either. Breaking a promise we made those many years ago negates the reason we took the time to bury something like a time capsule in the first place. Hell, I don't even remember what I put in there. Do you?

DANIELLE
(Shakes her head slowly)

Not a clue. It's been so long ago. What, over thirty years since we did that? A lifetime ago.

PERRY

Sure has been. You know, I almost had Mom and Dad talked into selling this place last year. But they decided not to.

DANIELLE

Why were you trying to get them to sell it?

PERRY

Property taxes are insane out here, and it's not worth spending money on something you ain't doing anything with. When I was married to my first wife and when our kids were younger, we would come out here a few times a year.

My new wife and I don't feel like driving all the way out here. We just relax at home. Mom and Dad haven't been out in years, I bet. Now, it just sits. A place like this is meant to be enjoyed.

DANIELLE

First wife? How is marriage this time around?

PERRY

Third time is a charm, they say, right? It's going better than the first two, I can safely say that for sure. What about you?

DANIELLE
(Pause, looks around)
I'm just a woman who puts being a doctor above everything else

PERRY

I thought you were married. At least that's what your Facebook status says.

DANIELLE

Jayson and I are currently in a gray area.

PERRY

What does the gray area mean?

DANIELLE

Means that he moved out a while back. I don't blame him.
I would've left me too.

PERRY
(Silence)
How long you two been married?

DANIELLE

15 years.

PERRY
(Silence)
Have you two made any decisions on your futures?

DANIELLE
(Silence)
Not really. He moved out, thinking that would provoke me
into making some grand declaration of my love and fight for
him to stay. But I let him go. Truth is, I didn't care if he
went.

PERRY

Was it a bad marriage?

DANIELLE

No, Jayson is a good man. Hard-working, intelligent, loyal,
honest. He's everything a woman wants in a person.

PERRY

So, what was the problem?

DANIELLE
*(She thinks it over for a few moments
before she answers)*

DANIELLE (Cont.)

You know, I don't really know. You ever have that feeling that something isn't right, but you can't define it? But deep down, you can feel it. And it's there, and you can't say precisely what it is, but you know something isn't right.

PERRY

Yeah, I do. It happened to me with my first wife, Angie. I knew that I shouldn't have married her. There was something about her that I couldn't place my finger on, much like you. But it was there nagging at me, and it sucks because you can't say exactly what it is. It's like an unease.

DANIELLE

Yeah, an unease. That's right. Like you have a weird sense of this is not where you're supposed to be kind of thing.

PERRY

Exactly. I think we just defined your feeling.

DANIELLE

I think you're right.

PERRY

How long you felt this way about him?

DANIELLE

Almost the entire time we were married.

PERRY
(Silence)

You know, growing up, I always thought you and Matthew would end up together. We all did, as a matter of fact; it just seemed like it was meant to be. You lost him, he lost you, and then that night here at the lake house after graduation...we thought it was going to be you two.

DANIELLE
Yeah, so did I. But things went in another direction.

PERRY
(Silence)
He really loved you, you know. Like he always did. Even when we were kids and he would never come out and tell us you two were dating, you know, back when y'all thought we didn't know, we knew *(Laughs),* but we all could tell.

DANIELLE
How could you tell?

PERRY
We could see the way the two of you looked at each other when we were all out doing stuff. We all knew. We just let you guys have your time. I know, we were actually decent for a change. *(Laughs)*

I remember when you guys broke up that time during junior year. You started dating that dude from the football team. It shattered Matthew. I mean, he was crushed.

DANIELLE
I only did that because he started talking to that Casey Kennedy girl.

PERRY
Oh yeah, I remember her. She was gorgeous. Wasn't she this uptight senior who was president of the debate team or whatever?

DANIELLE
That was her. She was also on the golf team and ran cross-country. I always hated her, and Matthew knew it. That's why he was with her.

PERRY

Well, he never took it beyond talking, so as you know. He still loved you.

DANIELLE
(The two of them sit and don't say anything for a few moments)
It was always Matthew. I guess it will always be.

PERRY
(Silence)
Do you want to go to the lake house and hang out? I'm getting a little stiff sitting out here—pitfalls of getting older.

DANIELLE

Sure, let's go.
(PERRY gets up and pulls DANIELLE up. The two walk up the dock, closing the scene)

End Scene 6

Act II

Scene 6

Tommy's old backyard. They have been digging holes for what seems to be hours.

TOMMY

Maybe it's right here?

> *(TOMMY takes the shovel and starts*
> *digging yet another hole)*

WARREN

Let's hope so. This is hole four now and nothing. How can we be this off? It's twenty-five paces, right? That's what Matty walked off back then, I remember.

TOMMY

Yeah, maybe we've been taking longer strides than his 13-year-old legs. I don't know.

WARREN

Maybe we're off the line of sight towards the house by a few feet either way. It's bound to be here. Maybe we'll get lucky, and that hole you're digging right there is where it's at.

TOMMY

What we need is a metal detector.

WARREN

You know, I didn't even think about that.

TOMMY

I didn't either until we'd dug up the whole backyard. Man, that would've come in handy.

WARREN

We'll switch out if we have to dig another one.
(WARREN watching TOMMY dig)

Does it feel weird being back in your old backyard?

TOMMY
(Digging)
Yeah, a little bit. Brings back some memories for sure. Like over there was where my basketball goal was. How many games did we all play there? Hundreds? And over there was where we all used to camp out in that big old tent back in the third and fourth grades. We thought we were men back then. (Laughs)

WARREN

Golden times, man, golden times. I remember playing football in this backyard with an orange Nerf ball. You could catch that thing with one hand and grip it without fumbling.

TOMMY

(Laughs) Yeah, that thing was awesome. I could throw that thing two hundred and fifty yards, I bet. Remember that green one that Perry had that glowed in the dark, and we'd come out here and play night games?

WARREN

Man, yes! That was awesome! God, we didn't know how good we had it as kids, did we?

TOMMY
(Digging)
Nope. No kids do, don't reckon. But being a kid back then, back in the late 80s and early to mid-90s was something special, wasn't it?

WARREN

Most definitely. It was before cell phones, social media, and the internet. Man, could you imagine if that stuff were around when we were kids?

TOMMY
(Digging)
We wouldn't be right here digging up a time capsule, that's for sure.

WARREN

Nope. We'd never gotten out of the house. Probably would've never been friends at all.

TOMMY

I'd say you're right about that. Man, you think about it, we were born at the right time in history.

(Silence as TOMMY is digging between the two men)

WARREN
Hey, I want you to know that I'm sorry we ain't as close as we were back when we were growing up and during high school.

TOMMY
(Digging)
No need to apologize, man. It's life. Nobody meant to drift away. The only ones who stayed in this town were Matty and you. We all left you guys behind. I should be sorry. I didn't keep in touch as much as I should have. That's on me.

WARREN
That's a two-way street. I could've been a lot more accessible with you all instead of being restricted to just liking Facebook posts and commenting here and there when you guys would post something. It's a damn shame that we all finally got back together because of Matthew's death and this box.

TOMMY
(Digging)
Well, in a way, Matty did bring us all together, right? Hell, I've enjoyed seeing you and spending time with you today. I just wish it were under different circumstances. Really wished Matty was here. I can hear him right now: 'Are you guys stupid? You mean to tell me you can't find a metal box'? *(Both men laugh)*

WARREN
And I can hear him saying that too. God, he was such a good guy, you know it?

TOMMY
(Digging)
The best friend a kid could ask for, I know that. I remember this one time that Jeremy Rider fouled me hard at the basketball court behind the bank in town. Now, you remember Jeremy, was about three inches taller than me, outweighed me by a good fifty pounds, and liked to fight.

WARREN

When was this?

TOMMY
(Stops digging)

This was summer of '94. I don't know where y'all were that evening, but it was just me and Matty shooting ball behind the bank, and Jeremy rolled up on his bike and wanted to play. We weren't going to tell him no, so we let him play.

Well, we're out there playing 21 when I got fouled hard going in for a layup by Jeremy. I mean, he knocked me down in midair, and I hit the concrete and banged my head against it. I saw stars.

Well, Matty saw it and got right up in Jeremy's face, and the two started mouthing off to each other. It was the first time I'd seen Matty that way, and the first time I'd seen Jeremy back off. He helped me up from the concrete, and the two of us went into Wilson's Drugstore to get a Pepsi and sit in the booth. God, he was mad about what Jeremy had done. I think he would've worn him out if Jeremy threw a punch. Never saw Matty that mad.

WARREN

That's crazy. I never heard that story before. I remember one time that me and Matthew went to the swimming pool and Lacy Holder was there.

TOMMY
(Back to digging)

Not THE Lacy Holder?

WARREN

Yup, that'd be her. The love of my teenage life. So anyways, me and Matthew were at the swimming pool and she's there and of course I ain't got the manhood to talk to her.

But y'all knew how I felt about her—talked about her endlessly.

So, there we were, and I started talking about her, how much I liked her, and all the other things. Matthew had gotten tired of me talking about her over the years, and he decided that he was going to go over and talk to her for me.

That's what he does. He walks right over there to where her, Erin Brooks, and Mandy Drummer were sitting by the fence, sunbathing. He starts to talk to her. By the time he comes back over to me, I'm a nervous wreck. But you know what? He got her phone number for me, and he had found out that she liked me, too.

                    TOMMY
                  (Digging)
And you guys dated for a little bit, right?

                    WARREN
We sure did. First girl I ever kissed and got to third base with. All because of Matthew. Had he not gone over there and talked to her that day, I would have never been with her. Man, looking back, he was something else.
          (Just then, TOMMY's shovel hit something metal)

It's the box!!
          (TOMMY starts to dig faster and faster)

                    TOMMY
Dude! We found the box! It's here!

End Scene 7

Act III

Scene 1

Inside the lake house.

DANIELLE, PERRY, WARREN, and TOMMY are all sitting in the living room/kitchen area of the lake house around the kitchen table. On the table is the metal box still wrapped in dirty plastic.

PERRY

I don't know about you, but this is kinda spooky in a way.

TOMMY

Yeah, like the last time we had eyes on this box was when Matty was alive. Seems like he should be here for this. Feels...off, I guess.

WARREN

I need a drink. Perry, I only assume there's still liquor around here.
                    (Gets up and prowls around the kitchen)

PERRY

Yeah, right side of that cabinet there. While you're at it, get four glasses. I have a feeling we all need something about now.

(The three sit around in their positions, looking at the metal box in clear heavy plastic sitting on the table. WARREN is making noise as he gets the drinks ready for himself and everyone. He brings each one their drink, but before anyone can take a sip, WARREN holds up his glass, causing the others to do the same)

WARREN

This is for Matthew. I already miss him.
(The others nod and take a sip just as WARREN does)

PERRY

The last time we were all here together was what? May 30th, 1997?

DANIELLE

Graduation night.

TOMMY

28 years ago. How did that happen?

WARREN

More importantly, how did time go by so fast? It's like we were kids and then BAM! We're here. I can't hardly account for the last nearly three decades.

PERRY

Deadlines and commitments. We are ruled by a calendar that takes our time.

DANIELLE

The busier you are, the faster it goes. I remember back when I was a kid, the old people used to tell me that time gets faster the older you get. Boy, they weren't lying, were they?

TOMMY

Absolutely not. Can you believe that we've made it to 47? I can't.

WARREN

I remember thinking when I was a kid that 47 was old. And now here we are.

PERRY

Do you feel old?

DANIELLE

I don't. I still feel pretty good. But I will say that menopause is starting to creep up on me.

TOMMY

I'm having to go to the bathroom to pee twenty times a night now. And I have to stand there and actually try to. They certainly don't tell you that in the life brochure, do they?

WARREN

But you guys still look good. I saw Timmy Washer the other day, and he looks like hell. I mean, he looks like he's 70.

DANIELLE

Well, Timmy always ran pretty hard back in high school, I remember. I doubt that changed any as an adult.

PERRY

I remember one time he and Matty raced down 411 highway before it became four-lanes. *(Laughs)* I was riding shotgun with him that night, and we're at the Rocky Top getting some chips and Cokes...

TOMMY

When was this?

PERRY

Oh, *(Thinks for a moment)* I want to say right when we all started driving. He drove his mom's Ford Taurus to school and around on weekends. Remember that car? Anyways, we're in the store getting our stuff, and it's late. It's eleven or so, and in walks Timmy with Steve Kline. Both of them were motorheads, if you remember.

So, Timmy and Matty are in there talking, and I don't know how it got to racing, but before I knew it, Matty and Timmy are going to race their cars down the highway. Of course, I think this is crazy, but what the hell, Matty was committed. I remember asking him when we were driving up there what was on the line if he won or lost. He said, 'Nothing, I just want to beat him with a granny car.'
(Everyone laughs)

So, we get to the top of the hill about halfway on the highway, and we can see for miles. There are no headlights in sight. Timmy and Matty park beside each other. We all get out, making small talk, and they decide that the finish line is past the turn-off where the high school is. About a half mile where we're at, right?

So, we're all in our cars, revving our motors up and all this and that, and Timmy's friend is standing just in front of us with a flashlight. When he turns it on, that's when the race is on. That dude turns on the light, and here we go.

Matty has got that Ford Taurus going 90, fastest I've ever been in a car and the dash, the whole thing starts shaking like the damn thing is about to fall off.
(Everyone is laughing)

I turned around and I saw that we had Timmy's car beat until he must've hit a boost or something because that kid flew by us like we were standing still and we were doing 90 with that dash just about to fall! One of my favorite memories right there with him.

(The laughing winds down to silence)

He called me once and left a voicemail, and asked about how I was doing and such. I was so busy that I never called back. I just forgot; I didn't think about it until we were at the graveside service today.

(Everyone is laughing, winding down a bit. Then silence for a few moments)

TOMMY

Tell you guys a story I never told anyone. It happened back in '94. You all remember Daphne Decker, the girl I was on and off with for a little while?

(Everyone nods and says yeah)

Well, what you guys didn't know was that she had gotten pregnant. And man, that news leveled me. Here I am, a teenager, didn't have a job, no car, just trying to deal with life, and here she tells me that she's pregnant. So much was going through my head at that time.

Me and Matty had been shooting basketball down at the park, and we were walking home. I just broke down on him. Tears all over my face, I'm blubbering, trying to say how bad I've messed up. Matty asks what's wrong. I tell him, standing there in the street

After I'm done, tears all cried out, you know what he does? He hugged me, and that made me feel so good. He had no idea how much I needed that. After a minute or two, he pulls back and looks at me through those thick black glass frames of his and says, "It's going to be okay. We'll figure this out'.

DANIELLE
Wow...what happened?

TOMMY
Daphne ended up having a miscarriage early. The only people who knew were my parents, hers, and Matty. But he was there with me when I told my parents that night. Right there he was, sitting beside me on the couch. The biggest thing he ever did for me, and I never forgot it. He got me through a tough time.
(Everyone was silent for a few moments)

WARREN
When my parents and I moved here in town back in 1985, he was the first friend I made in the first grade. And being the only black kid in an all-white school wasn't easy. But Matthew came up to me that day on the playground, and I'll never forget it. He had Optimus Prime and Megatron, you know, the Transformers, and asked which one I wanted to be. I chose Prime, and we played in the corner of the playground, where no one could bother us for the entire recess.
(Laughs a little to himself in disbelief)

I think about that day sometimes and what it meant to me. I came from a school where half of it was black, and the other half was white. So, coming to an all-white school scared me a little bit because no one looked like me. But Matthew showed me kindness that day and after that...I never felt like I *didn't* belong when I met you guys, even more so.

I had that lunch with him fifteen years ago. I could've called him and checked in on him, but I never did. He called my cell phone and texted, but like you guys, I was always too busy to return it. I always meant to, you know? Time got away from me. He must've thought I was a real prick.

(A moment of silence)

What happened to all of us?

TOMMY

What do you mean?

WARREN

Like, what happened to our friendship? What happened to that sense of family we had?
(*Nobody spoke for a few moments*)

PERRY

Life, man. Time took it all.

DANIELLE

Maybe we weren't as good friends as we thought.

TOMMY

Well, that's a hell of a thing to say.

DANIELLE

Why?

PERRY

She's right. We all know she is. The last real night we had together was here in this house when we graduated from high school. Where have we been since? Matthew and Warren stayed here in town. Danielle moved, I moved, and so did Tommy. I didn't keep in touch with any of you. I mean, I tried here and there, and Facebook made it easier, but that doesn't count.

(The group goes silent for a few moments)

TOMMY

I don't even have any of your phone numbers in my phone. When we were kids, I had everyone's phone numbers memorized. I never thought there would be a day when I didn't have a relationship with y'all.

I got a text from Matty a few years ago, maybe six years if I'm being honest. He texted me 'Hey, man, was thinking about you. Hope things are good!' I didn't even text him back. I got too busy, and by the time I thought to do it, too much time had gone by, and I said, 'What's the point now'?

WARREN

Maybe we were just 'get by's' for each other back then. Maybe we were friends because we had to be. It's not like we needed each other to navigate adulthood. Look at us. We're each pretty successful in our own way, and it didn't require any of us to be in the other's life.

PERRY

'Get by's?'

WARREN

Like, maybe we had to have each other to make it through being kids and school. It doesn't mean that the friendships were fake; it just means that's what it was supposed to be.
(The group considers WARREN'S statement silently for a few moments)

TOMMY

I loved you guys back then, I know that much. Would've died for any of you.

DANIELLE

But now we're strangers, tied to a past we all shared. And the man of the hour is gone who tied us together back then.

PERRY

And his last act of friendship is that damn time capsule and a promise that we all made to come back.

WARREN

You know, part of me doesn't even want to open it.

DANIELLE

What I was thinking, too.
(Silence between the group for a few moments)

TOMMY

No. We've got to open it up. We promised him. It's the last good thing we can do for him.

WARREN

Danielle, when was the last time you talked to Matthew? You two were the closest of the group, having dated.

DANIELLE
(Sits and thinks)
A couple of nights ago.
(The guys sat there stunned, looking at her)

TOMMY

Seriously?

DANIELLE
(Nods, wipes tears away)
Yeah—Um...we were seeing each other for the last couple of years, off and on.

PERRY

Seeing each other? Like...what? Like how it sounds?

DANIELLE
*(Takes a deep breath, exhales, and shifts
around on her chair)*

I got this friend request from him on Facebook, and it really surprised me that, after all the years that had gone by, he remembered me. So, I accepted his request, and we started talking. Things felt like they did back when we left it all those years ago. I think we both knew we'd end up back together somehow. Eventually, I invited him out to my place in Alabama... and he came. And then...

WARREN

He was cheating on his wife with you?

DANIELLE
*(Speaks lowly, as if in deep thought
about the subject, measuring her words)*

Yeah, that's about the size of it, I guess. We weren't proud of it. It just kind of happened.

TOMMY

So, elephant in the room: why didn't you guys end up together back in the day? We all thought you would in the end. Was it heading that way, right?

DANIELLE
(Sits and thinks)

After we called it quits back in high school, we were always best friends. When I decided to leave for college in Alabama after we graduated, we tried it one more time. It worked really well, but the distance was too much for us.

I was going into medical school, and that meant more time for us to be apart because I had been accepted into a school in Arizona. We talked about him moving out there with me, and he just didn't want to leave home.

So... that was the end. I eventually got married, and he did, too. And now I'm here.
(Silence in the room)

PERRY
What was his married life like?

DANIELLE
Not good. He told me that she had cheated on him twice. The first time they went to marriage counseling, he thought that might've fixed it. She had done it about a year after their first son was born. So, he forgave that. Chalked it up to her self-esteem after the baby, and them still being young and making mistakes.

The second time was about three years ago. He told me that it nearly devastated him. She wanted to go to counseling again, and he just shut her down. He told me that he hadn't ever gotten over the first time, not really, and when the second time came, it knocked him out.

So, he was in a bad spot mentally. He was already consulting with an attorney about getting a divorce. She had no idea. We had planned to be together, get married, and live happily ever after, like we should've done years ago.

But now...that's gone. *(Silence)*

I know what you guys must think of me...
(The guys all shook their heads and waved her off)

WARREN
We're not here to judge you, Danielle. That was your and Matthew's business. Not ours.

PERRY

And don't worry. What has been said here tonight doesn't leave, right guys? You two are our best friends. *(TOMMY and WARREN nod)*

DANIELLE

Thank you, boys.

I don't think he harbored any ill will towards any of you. When we were talking, he always spoke fondly of you guys and the times y'all had together. He missed you, but he understood how life was. He still considered y'all his family.

WARREN

Was he still in banking, Danielle? That's what he was doing 15 years ago when I had lunch with him.

DANIELLE

Yeah, he had been with a bank here in town for the last fifteen years after leaving Pepsi. He seemed to love his job.

PERRY

He was a banker? I would've never guessed that in a million years.

TOMMY
(Looks at DANIELLE)
What was he like? I mean, I didn't know him as an adult.

DANIELLE

The same Matty we all remember. Just a grown-up version. He got married at twenty-two to Carrie. Raised two boys, Dylan and Raylan, and worked there at the bank as the branch manager.

(Some silence for a few moments before TOMMY spoke)

TOMMY

I remember when I was going to quit high school. Matty heard about it and came over to my house after he got off work and talked to me all night long about how stupid I was. Of course, I didn't listen to him, thinking I knew what I was doing.

But when I went in there to officially drop out, I couldn't do it. His words kept replaying over and over in my head. You know what got me the most? Him telling me that if I did it, he'd be disappointed with me.

For some reason, that bothered me so much. That was the reason I didn't drop out...it was because I didn't want to disappoint him.

PERRY

I remember him taking care of me when I was sick with the flu when Mom and Dad were out in Colorado. Remember that? Danielle, you came over with him, too, a few times. Eighteen years old, taking care of his friend who was sick. That was the kind of man he was...one that I like to remember, you know?

(Moment of silence passes, all of them reflecting on their time with MATTHEW and what their role was in MATTHEW's life, and he with theirs)

WARREN

We'd better get this box open. It's already dark outside, and I told the wife I'd be home an hour ago.

PERRY

Yeah, we'd better get to the main event.

(Everyone exhales deeply as the four of them situate themselves in the chairs at the kitchen table, looking at the

box wrapped in plastic. PERRY starts to unwrap the plastic, and TOMMY gives him his pocketknife to use. PERRY cuts and saws until the box is free before them. PERRY flicks the two latches and must force them open, and then prys the lid open with the knife. The lid flies open, and there are the contents of the time capsule waiting for them. Everyone reaches inside and retrieves the item they put in years ago. They were stunned, enamored of the items that had long been forgotten.

TOMMY
(Holding up a NES cartridge of Mike Tyson's Punch Out!!)

I totally forgot about putting this in here. Man, me and Matty played this game so freaking much! I never could beat Tyson at the end, though, but Matty claims he did while he was spending the night, and I was asleep.

PERRY
(Marveling over his Guns 'N Roses Appetite for Destruction CD in his hands)

God, I loved this CD. It was the first one I ever bought with my lawn mowing money. Hang on...let me see if it's still...
(Opens the case, and on the inside was a phone number written in marker)
I remember when I got Rachel Radkey's phone number, and I wrote it down on this insert so I wouldn't forget! Man, this is awesome!

WARREN
(Pulls a photo that was in a black frame out of the box. He holds it in his hands, marvling over it like the others were still doing their recovered treasures)

WARREN (Cont.)

Damn, look at all of us. We're so young! This picture was taken what, maybe back in 1989? Maybe 1990? I remember having my mom snap it. Tommy had that stupid buzz cut going on that time. *(Laughs)*

DANIELLE
(Takes the photo from WARREN's hands)
Oh my God! Look at my hair back then!

PERRY

Man, this is crazy! This is the only picture of all of us that was taken, right? I'd like a copy of this, please. *(Talking to WARREN)* Don't forget me.

DANIELLE
(Takes out her cat's collar, which had a name tag hanging from it. Mushroom was the cat's name. She held it in her hands and wept for her long-dead pet)

I loved this cat so much. I had forgotten about this being in here.

> *(The last item in the box is Matthew's Atlanta Braves baseball hat. He wore the hat everywhere he went before placing it in the time capsule. No one wanted to get it out, but they saw it sitting there, waiting for decades to be taken out)*

> *(DANIELLE puts her cat's collar down on the table and reaches into the box and slowly takes out MATTHEW's hat. Everyone watches and says nothing. She closes the lid to the metal box and lays the hat on top of it. Everyone stares at it for some time in silence, flooded by memories*

of the kid who wore the hat for so many
years during their childhood days)

TOMMY

He never went anywhere without that hat right there. I mean, he had another Braves hat after he put this one in the box, but he said this one held the most special memories for him.

WARREN

I can still see him wearing it.

PERRY

To this day, I can't see a Braves hat or shirt without thinking about him.

DANIELLE

I forgot he put this in here.
        (Some more silence between them all for
        a few moments)

WARREN

So...what are we going to do with the hat?

TOMMY
        (Looking at DANIELLE)
Seems fitting that you take it.

DANIELLE
        (Without hesitation, she takes it from the
        lid of the metal box and puts it up to her
        face and cries into it. Eventually, she
        puts it on her head and wears it)
Thank you, guys.

End Scene 1

Act III

Scene 1

Night

At the end of the dock, facing the audience, sits DANIELLE and MATTHEW. DANIELLE is wearing MATTHEW's Atlanta Braves hat.

MATTHEW
How was it seeing the boys again?

DANIELLE
It was good. Been a long time. Had some laughs, had some tears. But it was a good visit. I just wish it were under better circumstances.

MATTHEW
Yeah, I know. Sorry about that.
            (Puts his arm around her to comfort her)
It's a nice night out.

DANIELLE
Sure is.

MATTHEW

The stars look like they did that night you and I went to the park during Spring Break. You remember that?

DANIELLE

(Nods against his shoulder)
How could I ever forget? It was the first night we kissed.

MATTHEW

Yeah. What a magical night that was. You know, out of all the nights I've ever had in my life, that was one of the best. I never forgot it.

DANIELLE

Me either.

MATTHEW

I'm glad you have my hat now. God, I loved that thing as a kid. Never had a hat fit me like that one. *(Chuckles)*

DANIELLE

It's in good hands now forever.
(Silence for a few moments)
What am I going to do now?

MATTHEW

Anything you want.

DANIELLE

I don't know anymore. Your death has changed my future.

MATTHEW

A possible future. Not your *entire* future. You still have many years ahead of you, sweetheart. Don't waste your time, because life passes by so quickly. I had no idea my number was coming up last week. Had I known, I would've come down to spend the rest of my time with you.

(Silence between the two for a few moments)
MATTHEW (Cont.)
You remember the last time we were here on this dock?

DANIELLE
(Head on MATTHEW's shoulder, looking
out across the lake/audience, nods
against his shoulder)
Yeah.

MATTHEW
(Smiles)
Me too. Graduation night, after the guys all fell asleep up at the house, me and you came down here. We had that portable tape player with us. You set it down right over there behind us and hit play on the tape. You remember the song?

DANIELLE
(Nods against shoulder)
Of course. It was "Plainsong" from the Cure. It was our song.

MATTHEW
We slow danced to that out here under the stars, and we made all these declarations and predictions about the future as best and honest as 18-year-olds can do.

DANIELLE
I remember.

MATTHEW
(Silence between the two)
Danielle Watts...would you do me the honor of having one last dance?

DANIELLE
(Nods)

Yes.

(The two of them get up to their feet and embrace in a slow dance under the stars on the dock as the song from the Cure, "Plainsong", plays for 5 minutes)

(The stage lights slowly dim until the light is completely off and the curtain closes)

End of the play

Also by Matthew McConkey

Home Again, a novel
Scarecrows and Shadows, stories
Maple Lane, a novel
Everything Fades in Time, stories
Summerland, a novel
Far Away from Nowhere, stories

.

THE AUTHOR

Matthew McConkey is a novelist, fiction writer, and playwright. He is the author of three novels and three collections of short fiction. He lives in Tennessee.

www.ingramcontent.com/pod-product-compliance
Lightning Source LLC
Chambersburg PA
CBHW030505130626
46549CB00007B/2857